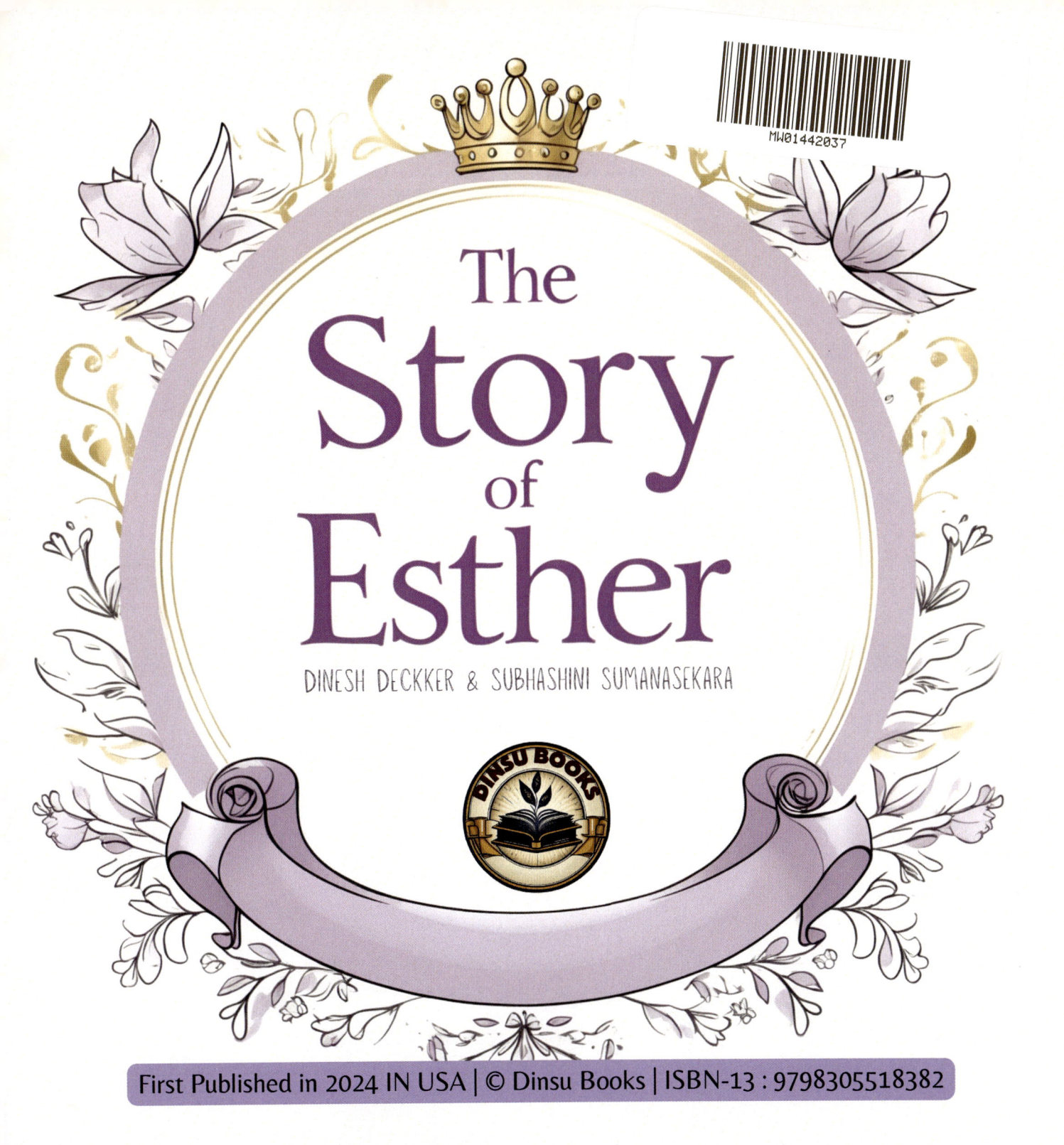

The Story of Esther

DINESH DECKKER & SUBHASHINI SUMANASEKARA

First Published in 2024 IN USA | © Dinsu Books | ISBN-13 : 9798305518382

Introduction

Esther was a brave and kind young woman chosen to be the queen of Persia. When her people, the Jews, were in danger, Esther stood up to save them. This story teaches us about courage, trusting God, and doing the right thing, even when it's hard.

THIS BOOK IS DEDICATED TO OUR PRINCESS SASHA.

What is Bible?

The Bible is a very special book that tells the story of God's love for everyone. It's like a big book full of stories, poems, and teachings that help us learn about God and how we should live our lives.

The Bible is made up of two main parts: the Old Testament and the New Testament. The Old Testament has stories about the world before Jesus was born, including the story of how God created everything and the adventures of God's people. The New Testament tells us about Jesus, His life, and the good things He taught.

Many different people, called authors, wrote the Bible over a long time. They were inspired by God, which means God helped them know what to write. Even though the Bible is very old, it still helps us today because it teaches us about love, kindness, and doing the right thing.

So, when we read the Bible, we can learn about God's amazing love and the stories of people who followed Him. It's like a guidebook that helps us understand more about God and how to be good and kind to others.

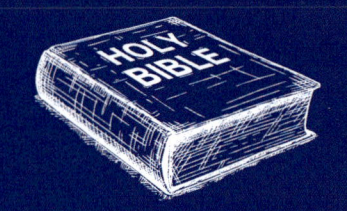

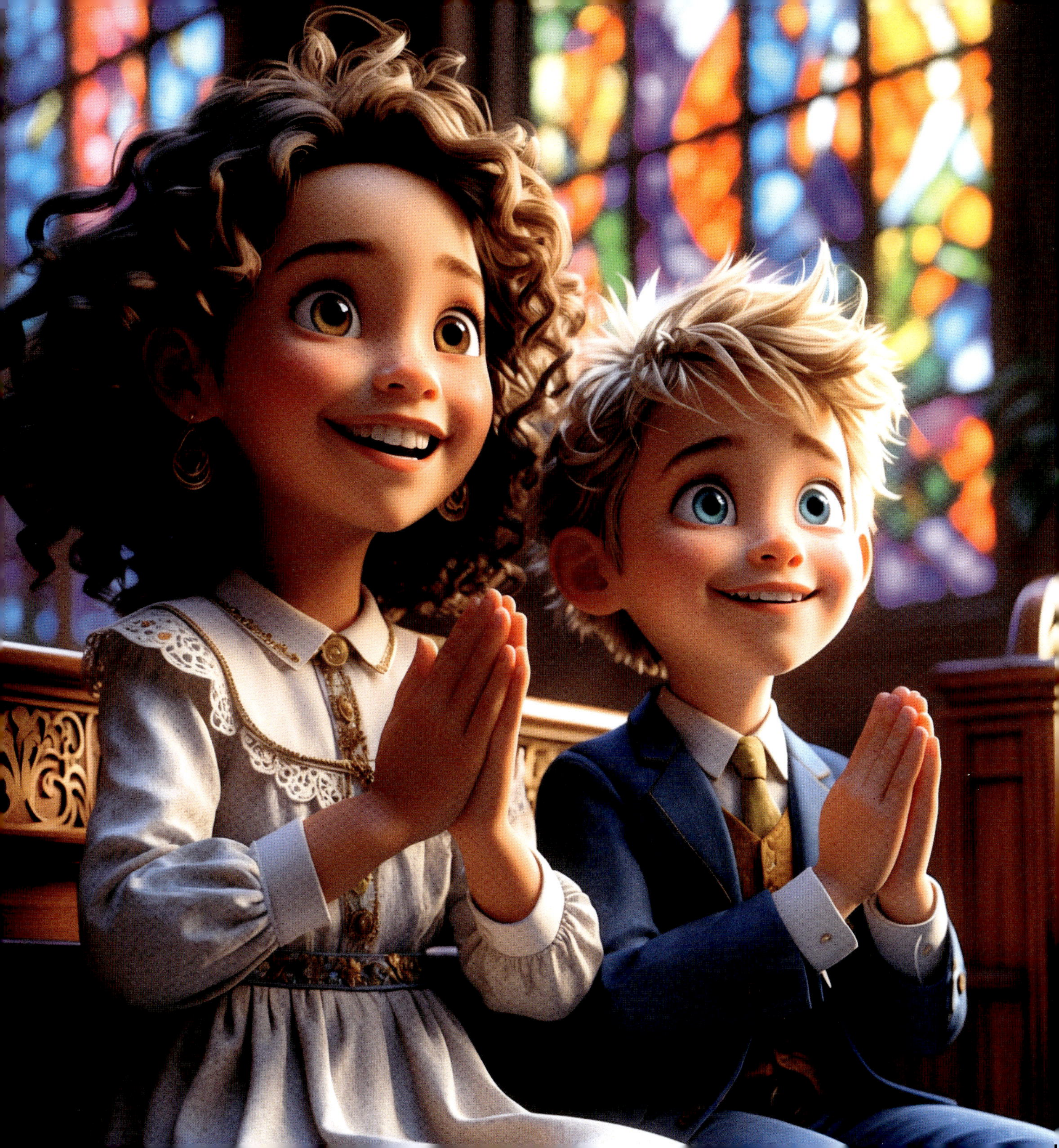

Chapter 1: Esther Becomes Queen

The king of Persia wanted a new queen. Esther, a kind and beautiful Jewish girl, was chosen.

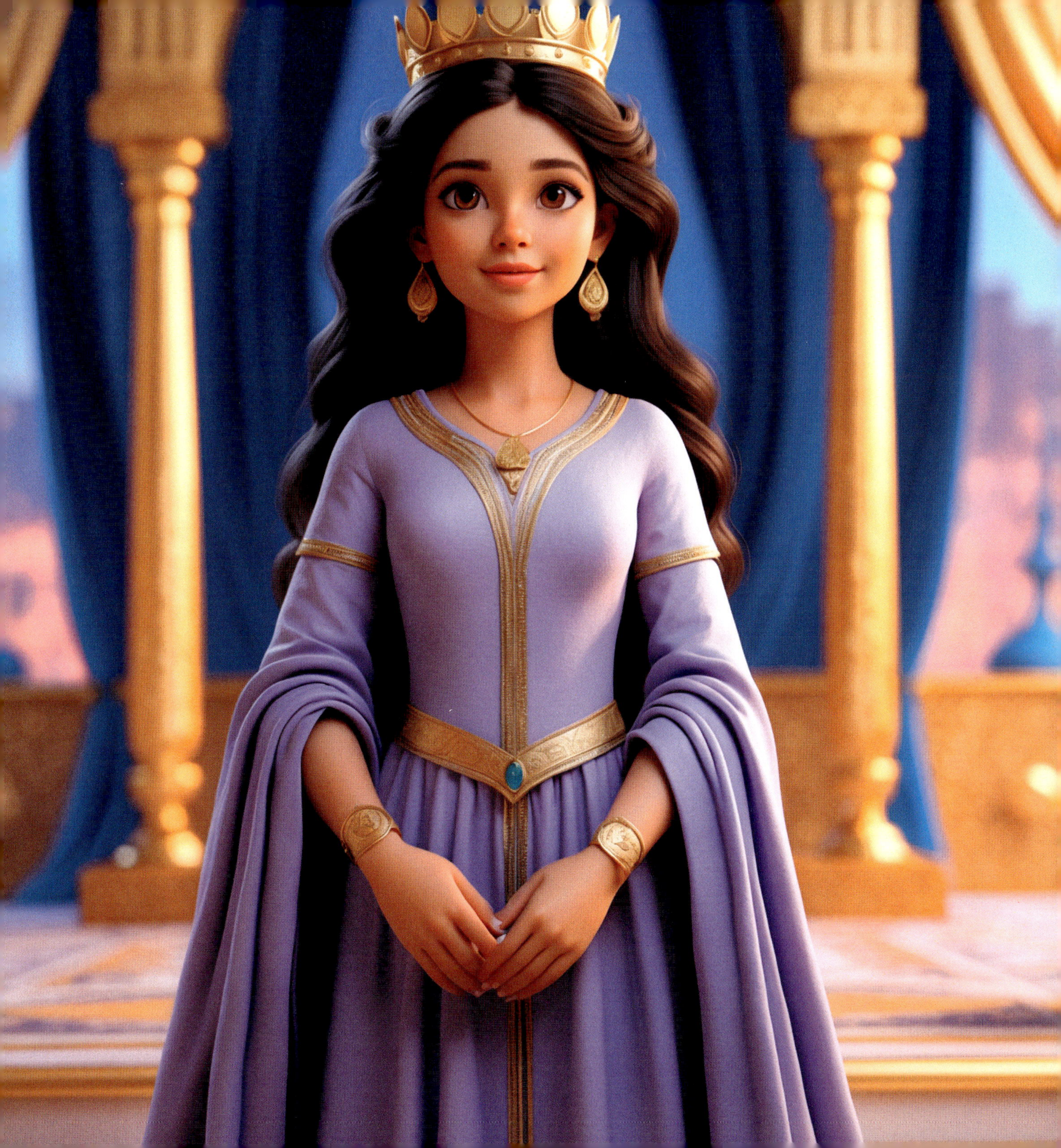

Mordecai's Warning

Mordecai, Esther's cousin, warned her not to tell anyone she was Jewish because it might be dangerous.

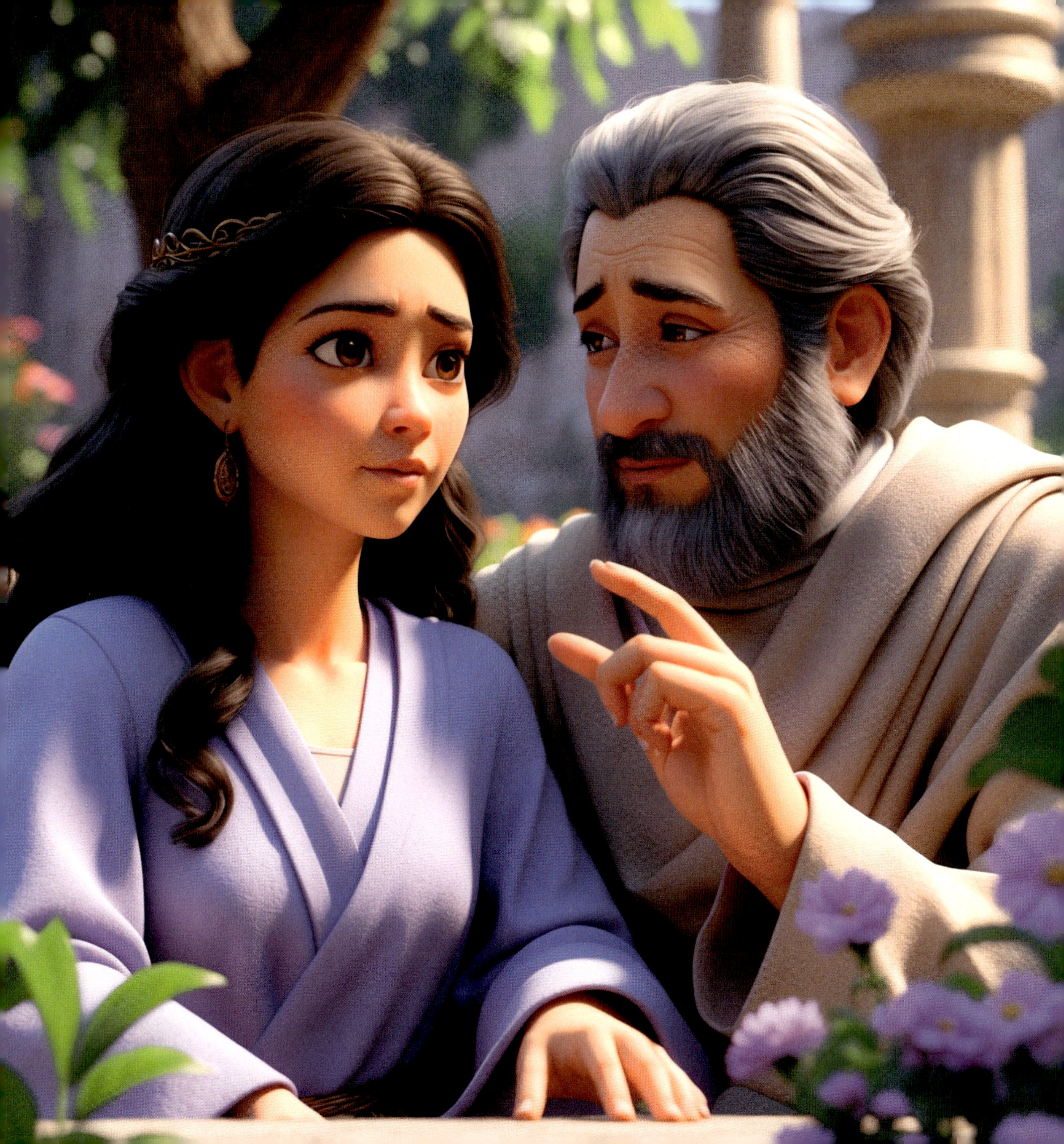

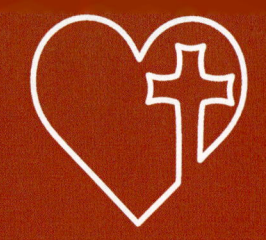

Haman's Evil Plan

Haman, an important man in the palace, made a plan to harm all the Jews because Mordecai wouldn't bow to him.

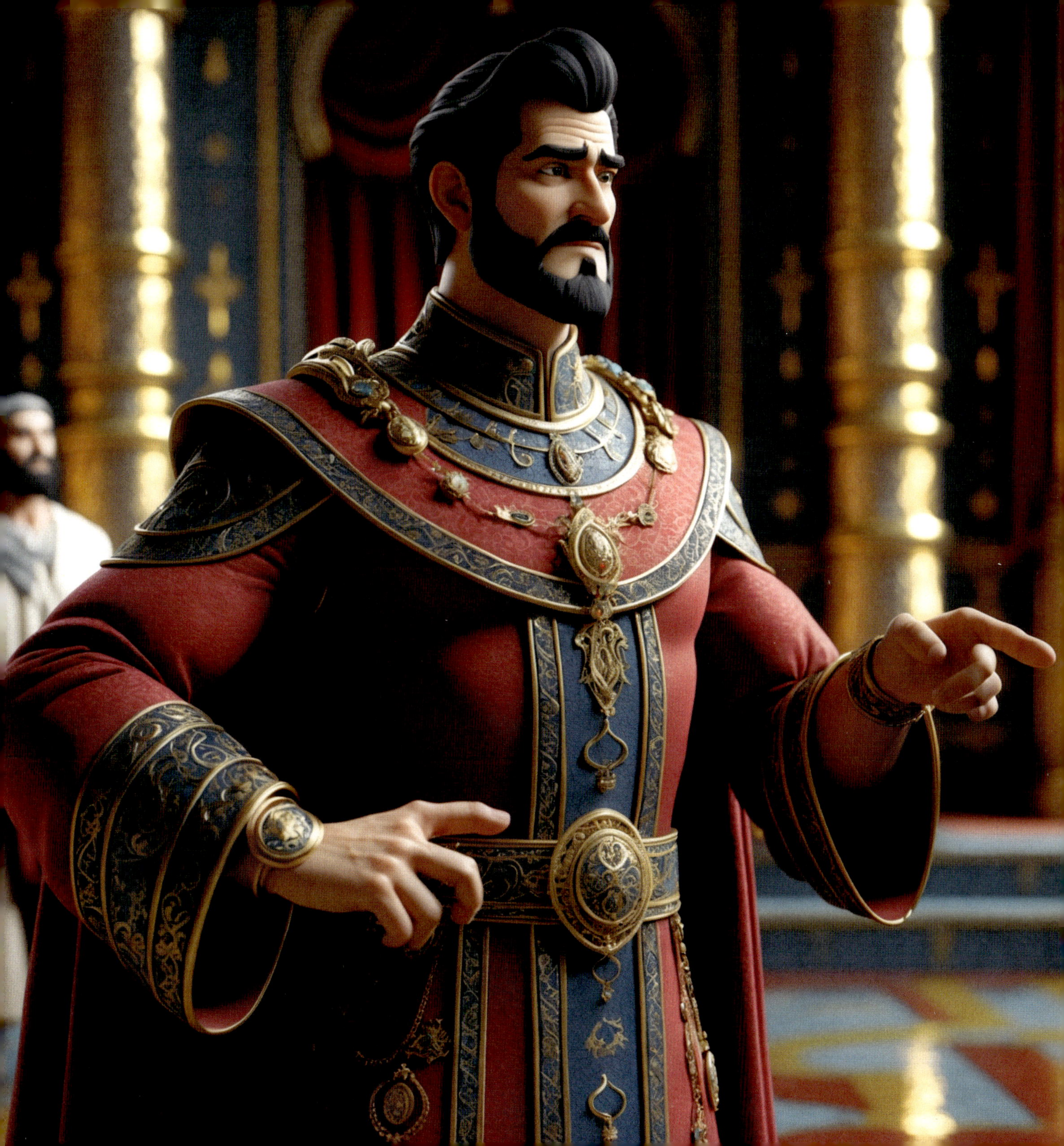

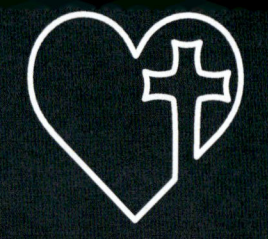

Mordecai Asks Esther for Help

Mordecai told Esther about Haman's plan and asked her to talk to the king. But Esther was scared because speaking to the king without being called could mean death.

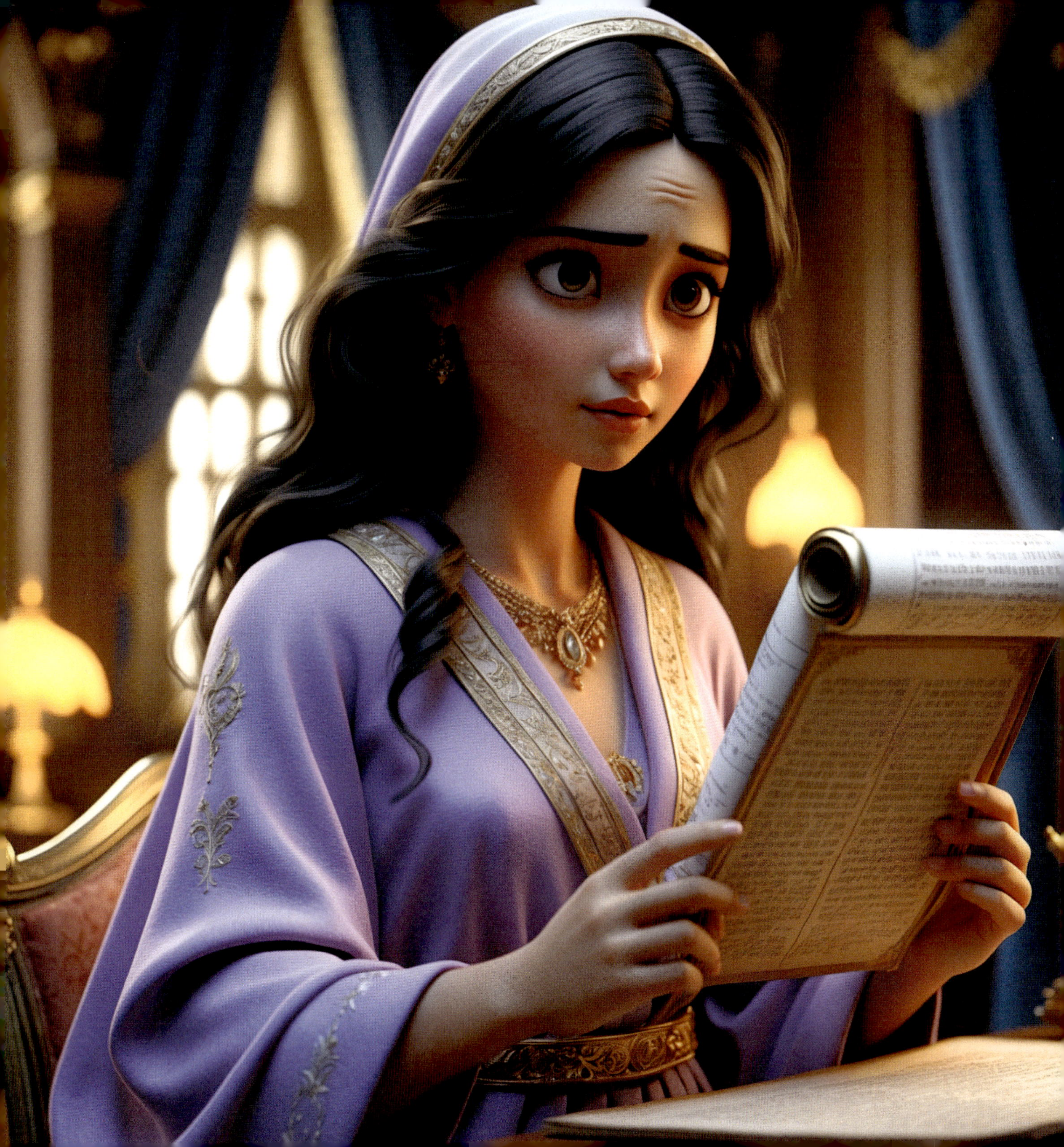

Esther Prays for Courage

Esther prayed and fasted for three days, asking God for help and strength to speak to the king.

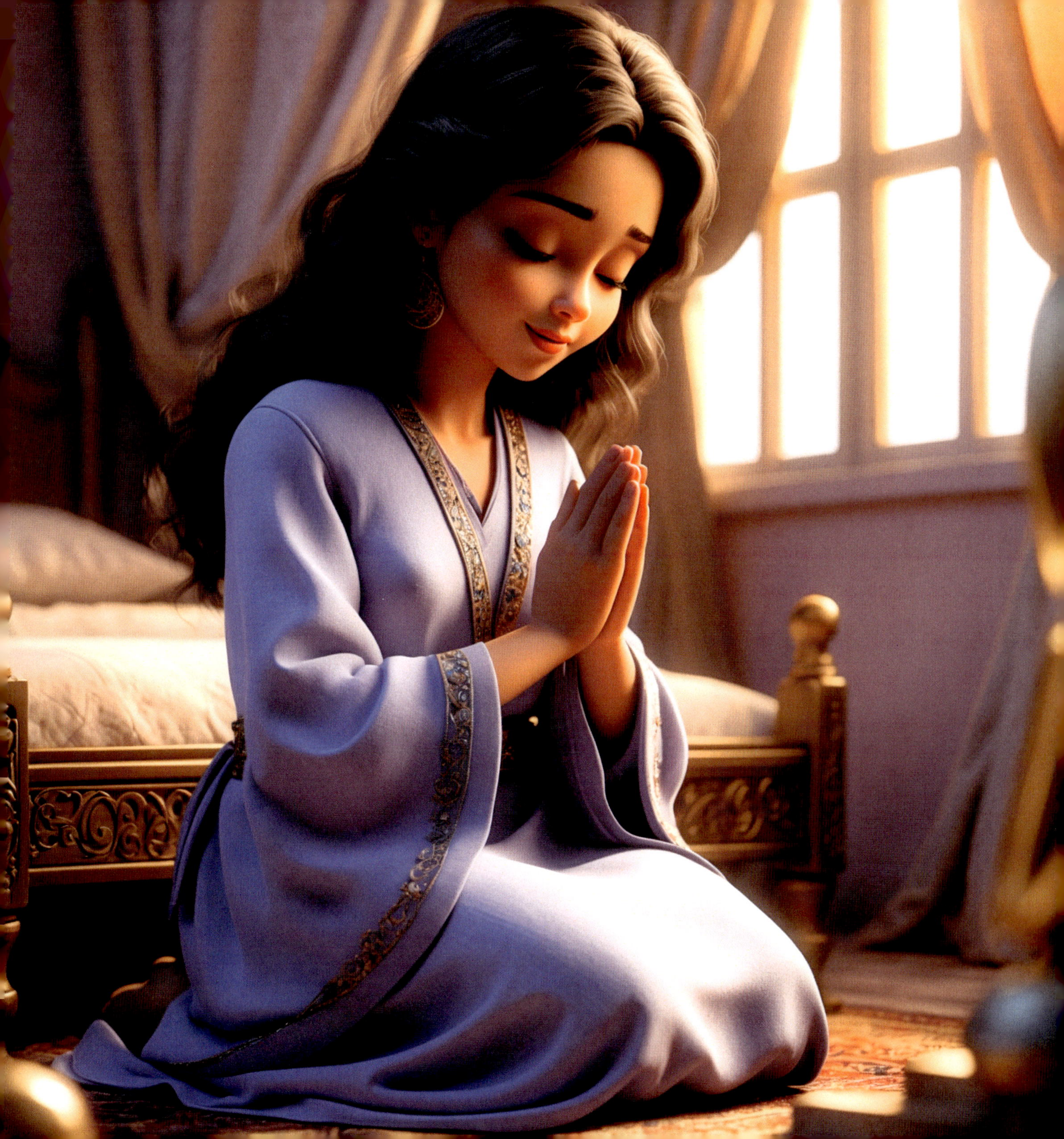

Esther Speaks to the King

Esther bravely went to the king, and he welcomed her. She invited him and Haman to a special dinner.

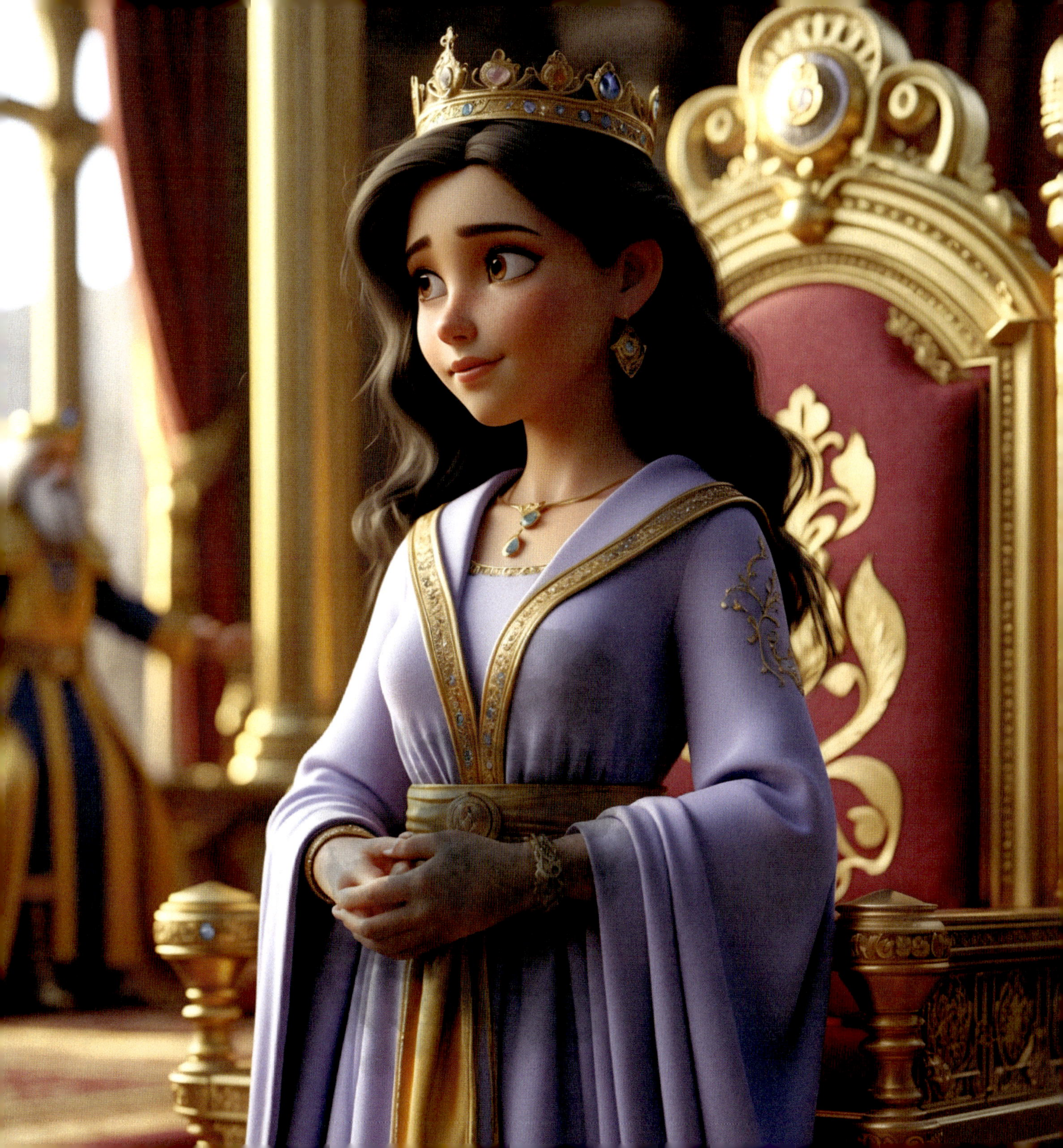

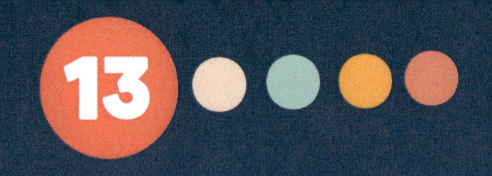

Esther Reveals the Truth

At the dinner, Esther told the king about Haman's evil plan and revealed that she was Jewish. The king was furious with Haman.

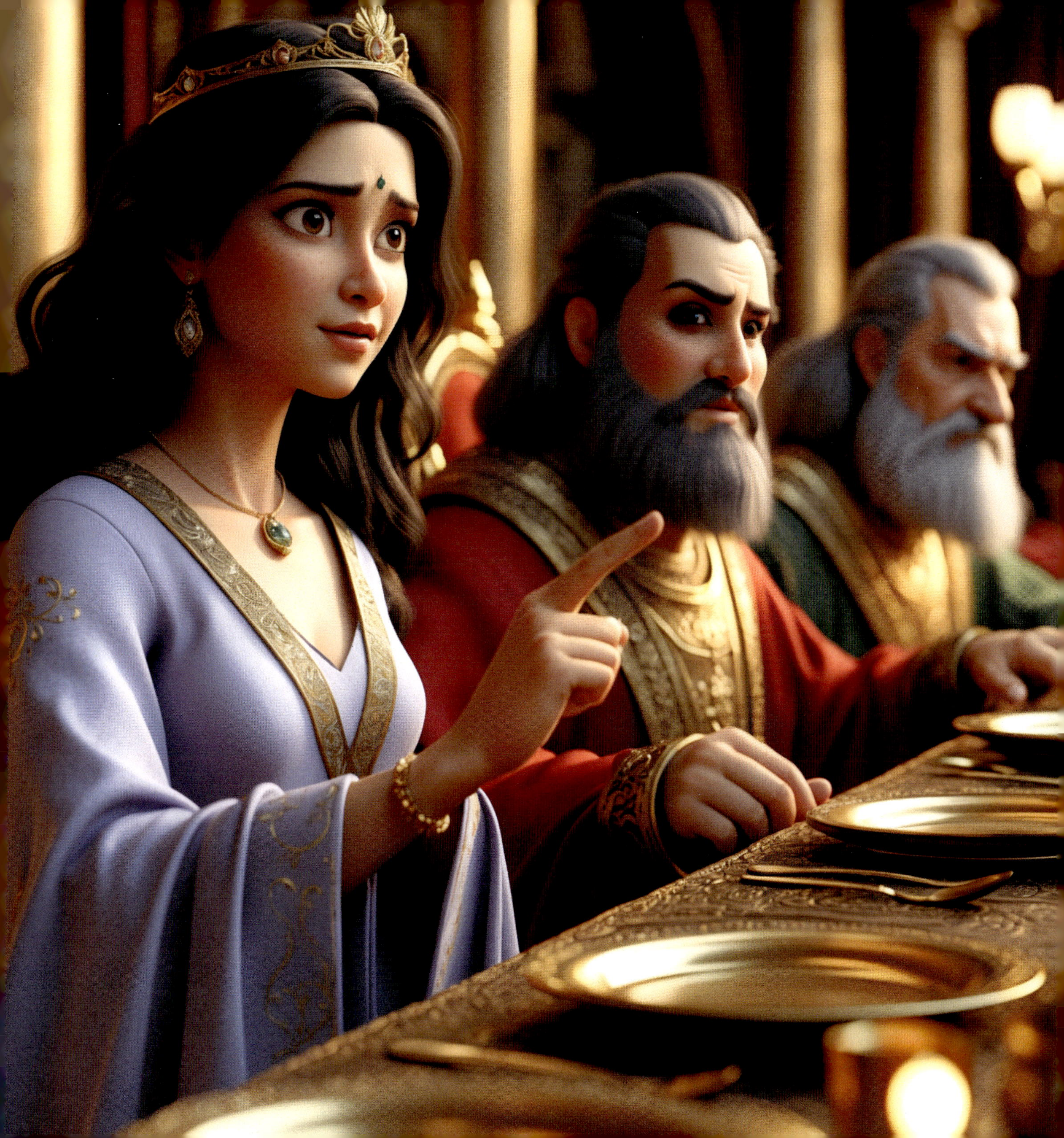

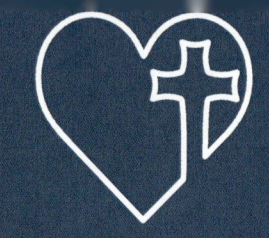

Haman is Punished

The king punished Haman for his evil plan and canceled the order to harm the Jews.

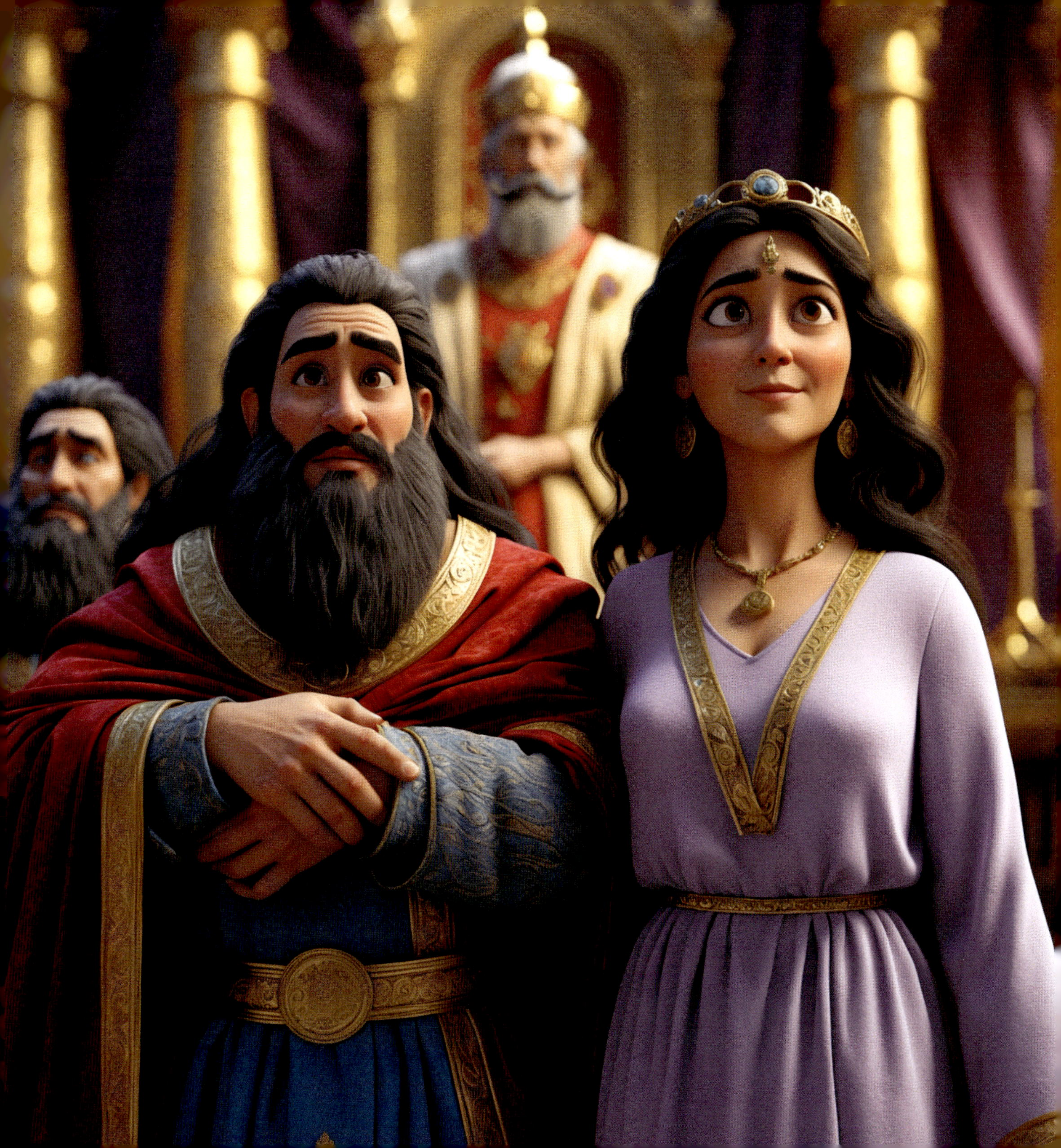

The Jews Celebrate

The Jews were saved, and they celebrated with joy, giving thanks to God for His protection.

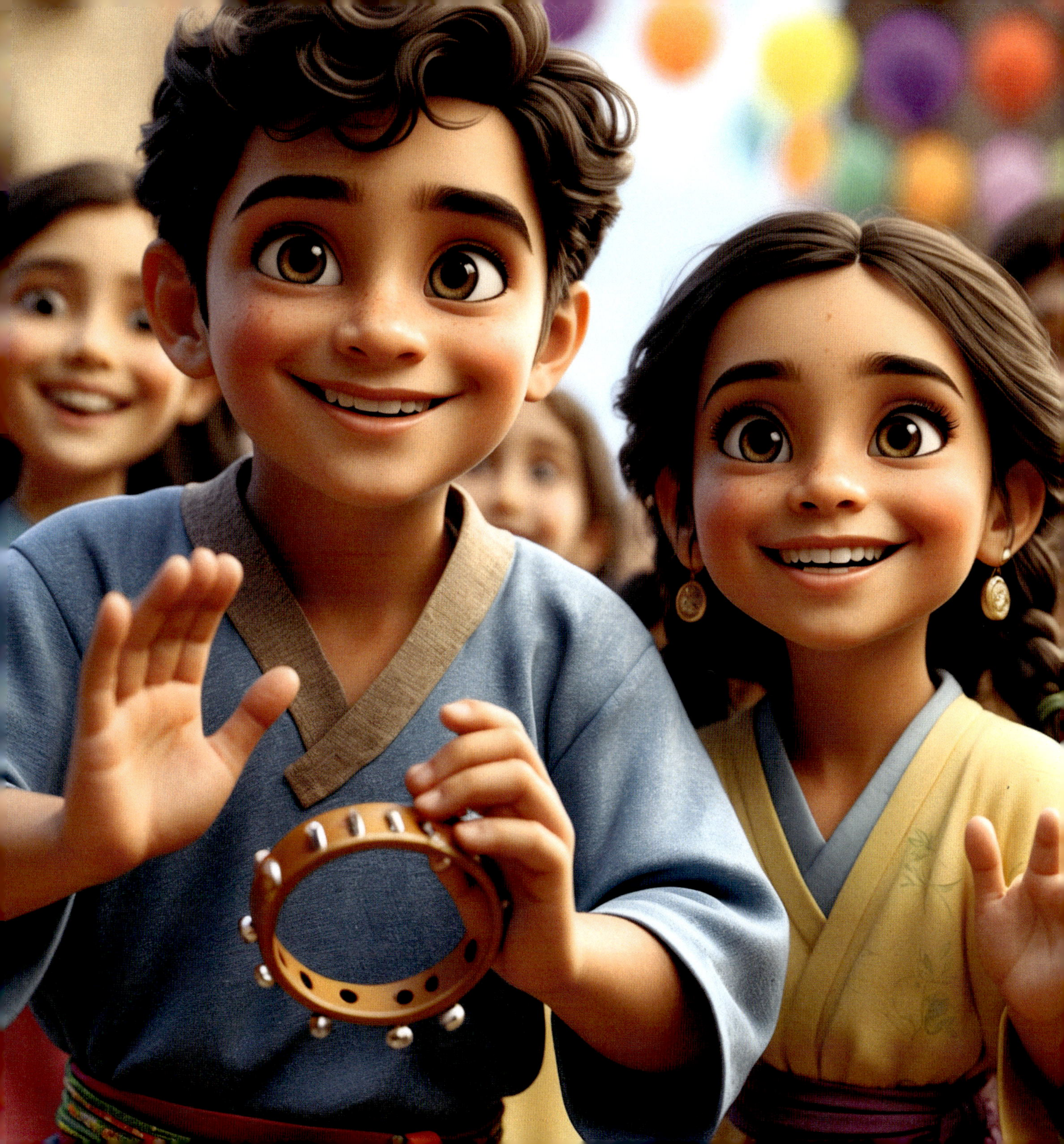

Esther's Legacy

Esther's bravery and trust in God saved her people. Her story reminds us that courage and faith can change the world.

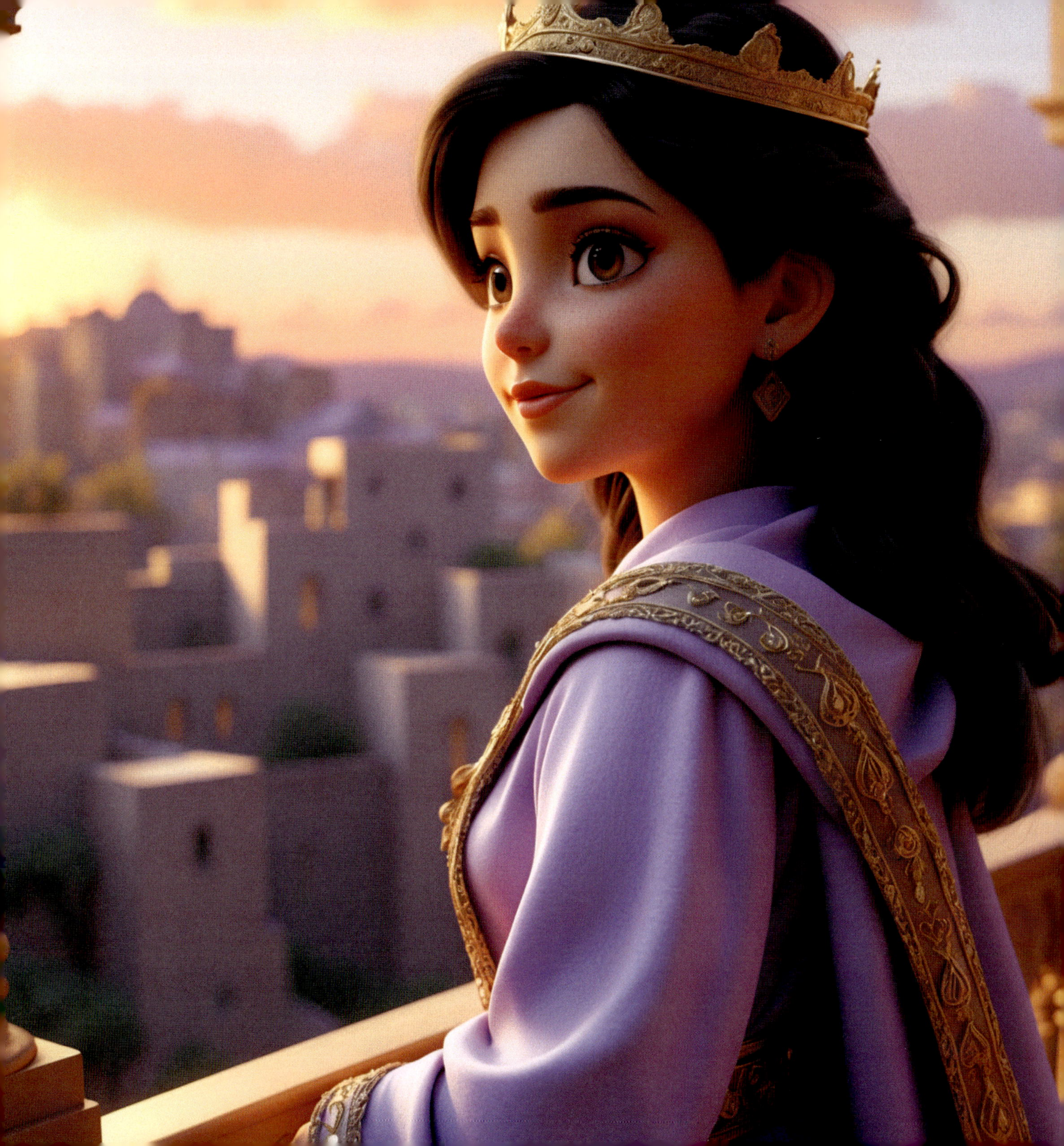

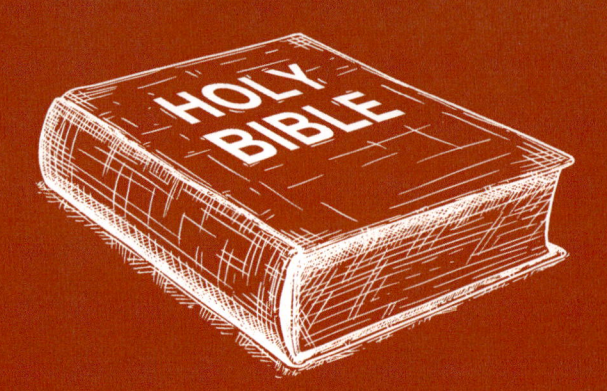

Hello, wonderful young explorers!

God has a plan for each of us. Esther's story shows us how faith and courage can make a difference. It reminds us to trust God, stand up for others, and do what is right.

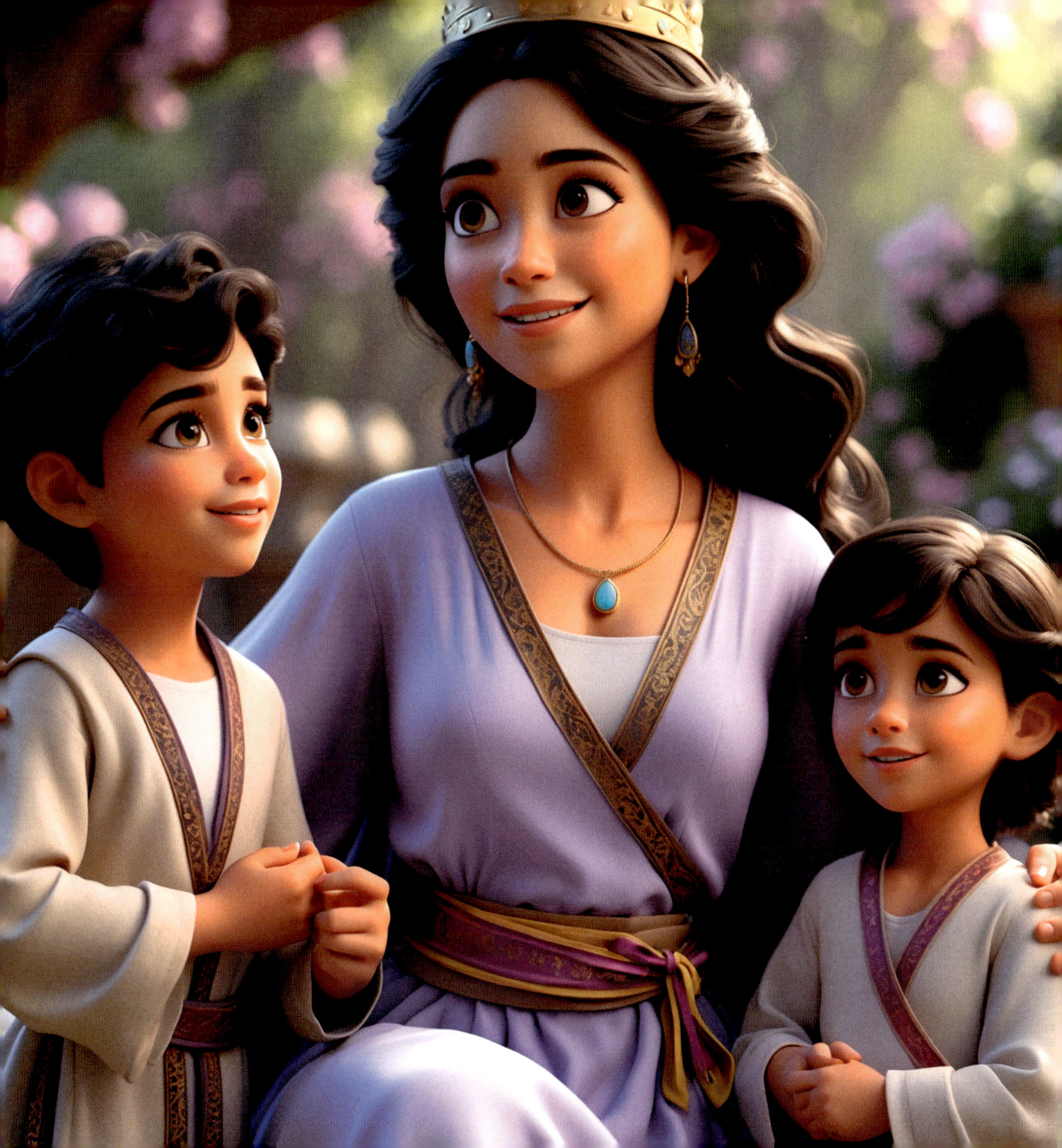

Questions for Children:

1. Who was Esther?
2. How did Esther become queen?
3. Why did Mordecai tell Esther to keep a secret?
4. Why was Haman angry with Mordecai?
5. What was Haman's plan?
6. What did Mordecai ask Esther to do?
7. How did Esther prepare to see the king?
8. What did Esther tell the king at the banquet?
9. What happened to Haman?
10. What can we learn from Esther?

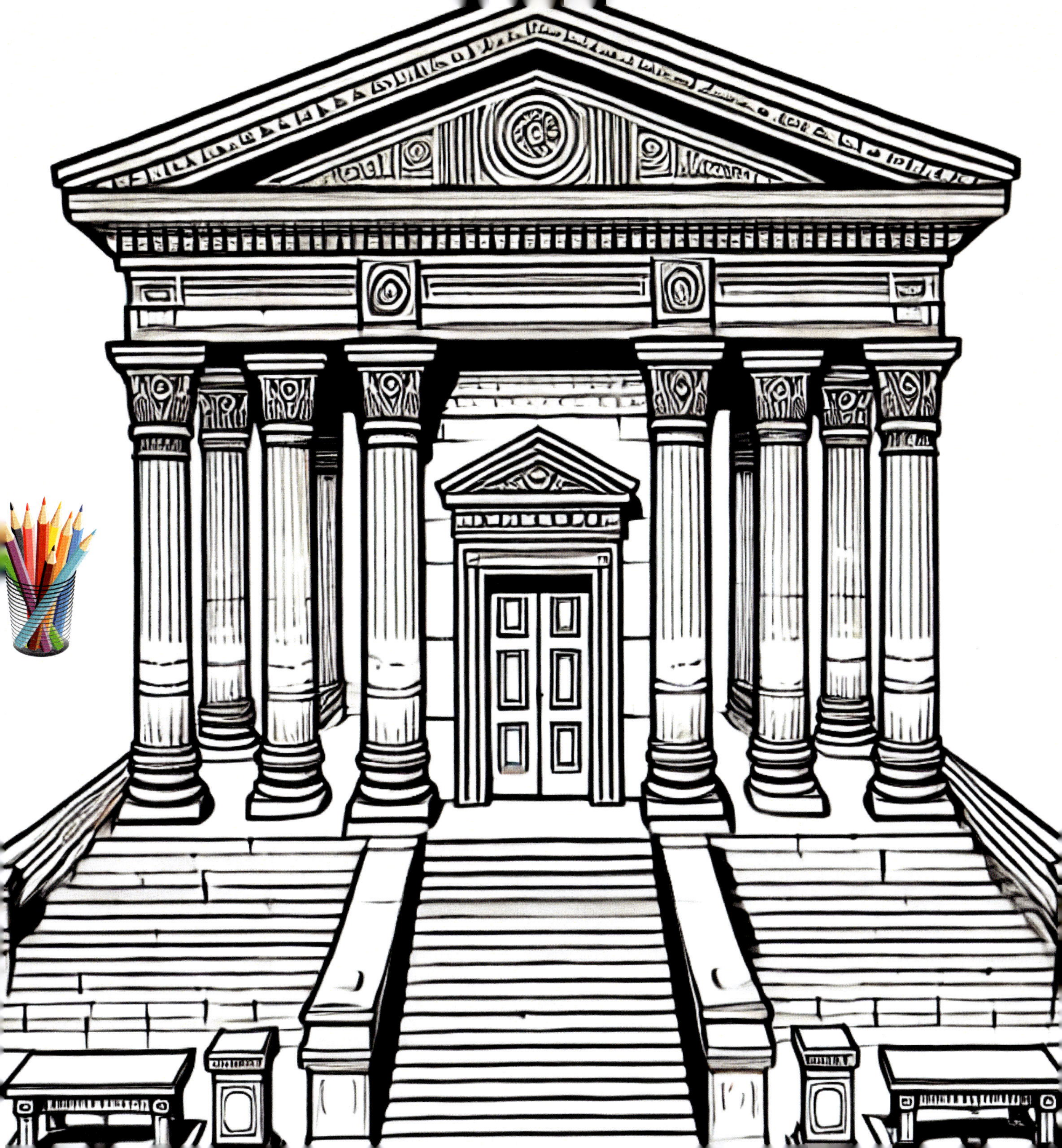

DINESH DECKKER
AUTHOR

Dinesh Deckker is a multifaceted author and educator with a rich academic background and extensive experience in creative writing and education. Holding a BSc Hons in Computer Science, a BA (Hons), and an MBA from prestigious institutions in the UK, Dinesh has dedicated his career to blending technology, education, and literature.

BA, MBA (UK), PhD (Student)

He has further honed his writing skills through a variety of specialized courses. His qualifications include:

- Children Acquiring Literacy Naturally from UC Santa Cruz, USA
- Creative Writing Specialization from Wesleyan University, USA
- Writing for Young Readers Commonwealth Education Trust
- Introduction to Early Childhood from The State University of New York
- Introduction to Psychology from Yale University
- Academic English: Writing Specialization University of California, Irvine,
- Writing and Editing Specialization from University of Michigan
- Writing and Editing: Word Choice University of Michigan
- Sharpened Visions: A Poetry Workshop from CalArts, USA
- Grammar and Punctuation from University of California, Irvine, USA
- Teaching Writing Specialization from Johns Hopkins University
- Advanced Writing from University of California, Irvine, USA
- English for Journalism from University of Pennsylvania, USA
- Creative Writing: The Craft of Character from Wesleyan University, USA
- Creative Writing: The Craft of Setting from Wesleyan University
- Creative Writing: The Craft of Plot from Wesleyan University, USA
- Creative Writing: The Craft of Style from Wesleyan University, USA

Dinesh's diverse educational background and commitment to lifelong learning have equipped him with a deep understanding of various writing styles and educational techniques. His works often reflect his passion for storytelling, education, and technology, making him a versatile and engaging author.

SUBHASHINI SUMANASEKARA
AUTHOR

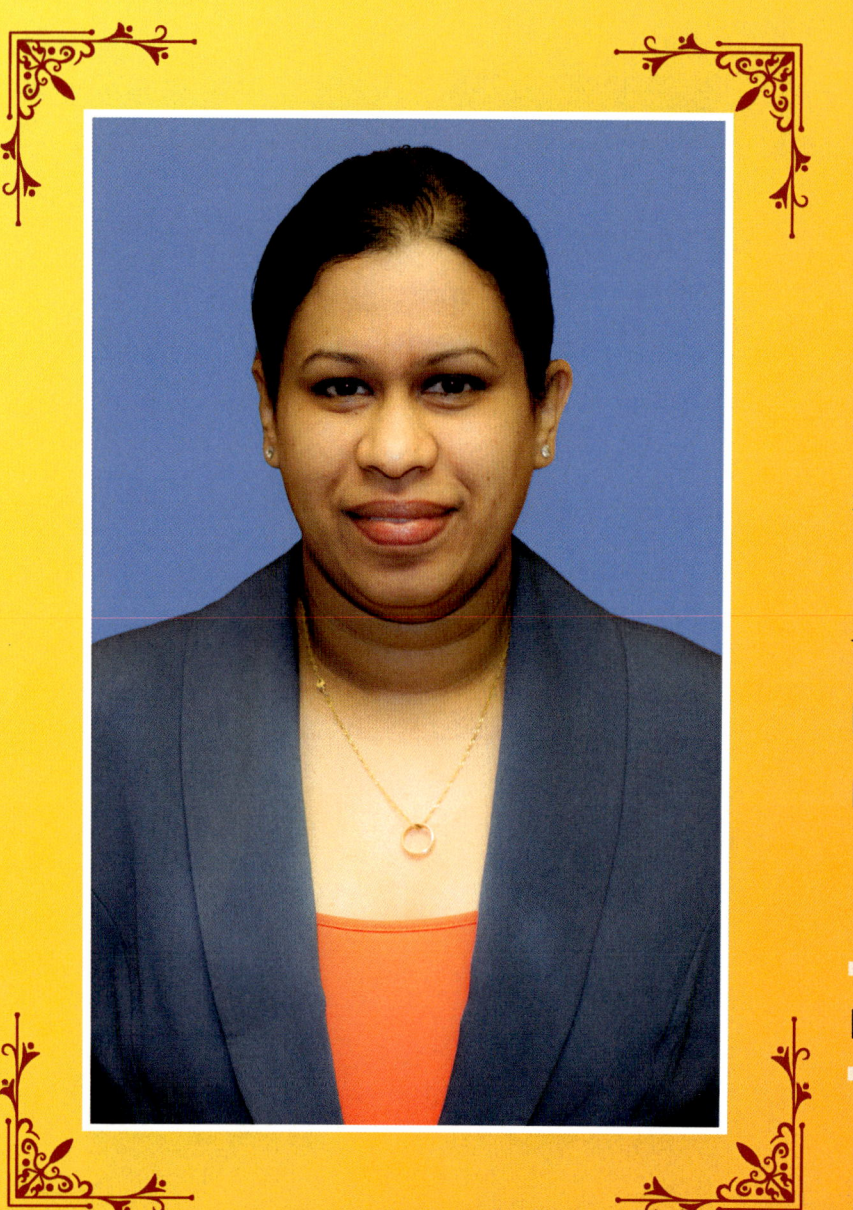

With more than 20 years of expertise, Subhashini Sumanasekara is a renowned ICT educator committed to mentoring students from a variety of backgrounds. Her experience in the industry is further enhanced by her Master of Science in Strategic IT Management.

BSc, MSc (UK), PhD (Student)